GUIDE TO
SWEDEN

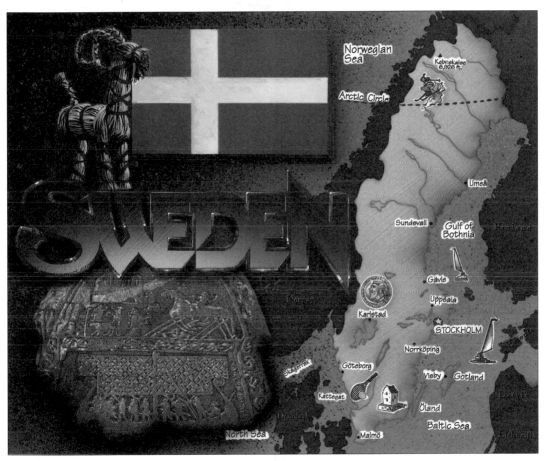

BRIAN WILLIAMS

Consultant: Gunilla Borén

Highlights for Children

CONTENTS

On the cover: Shown here is a sunset view of Old Town, part of Stockholm, Sweden's capital city. The city is built on fourteen islands.

The publisher is grateful for the guidance of the Swedish Tourist Office in London, England, and to Gunilla Borén of Borås, Sweden. **Gunilla Borén** is an assistant professor at the University of Borås, a critic, a writer, and a translator. She is also president of the International Board on Books for Young People (IBBY) in Sweden.

Published by Highlights for Children
© 2000 Highlights for Children, Inc.
P.O. Box 18201
Columbus, Ohio 43218-0201
For information on *Top Secret Adventures*, visit
www.tsadventures.com or call 1-800-962-3661.

10 9 8 7 6 5 4 3
ISBN 0-87534-573-5

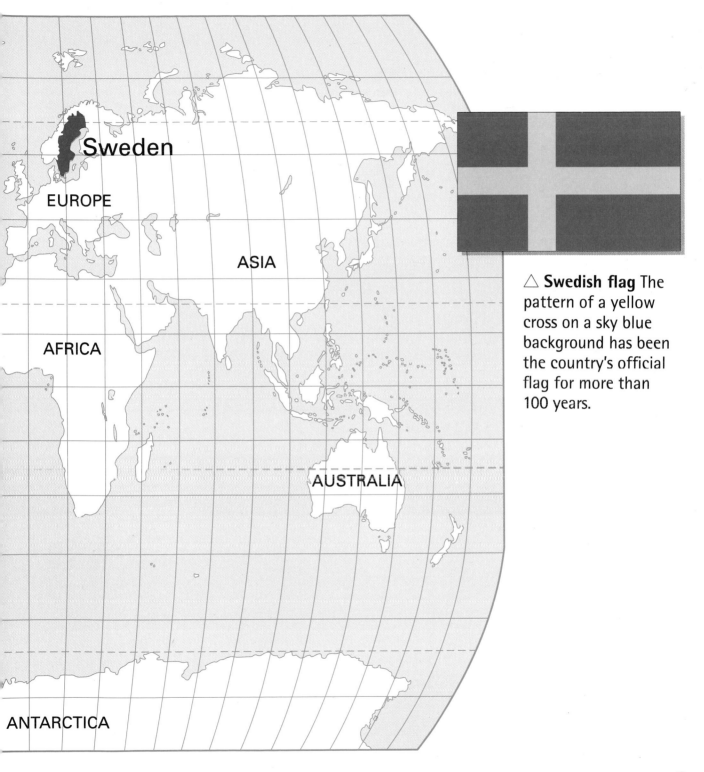

Sweden

EUROPE

ASIA

AFRICA

AUSTRALIA

ANTARCTICA

△ **Swedish flag** The pattern of a yellow cross on a sky blue background has been the country's official flag for more than 100 years.

SWEDEN AT A GLANCE

Area 173,732 square miles
(449,964 km^2)

Population 8,894,000

Capital Stockholm, population of city
and surroundings 1,588,000

Other big cities Göteborg (454,000),
Malmö (248,000), Uppsala (184,000),
Norrköping (124,000)

Highest mountain Kebnekaise,
6,926 feet (2,111 m)

Biggest river Göta alv (begins in
Norway), 447 miles (719 km)

Largest lake Lake Vänern,
2,156 square miles (5,585 km^2)

Official language Swedish

▽ **Swedish stamps** Two of the designs below show the building of the new bridge that links Sweden with Denmark. The other designs show some of the country's wildflowers, celebrations of Midsummer festival, and a crayfish party.

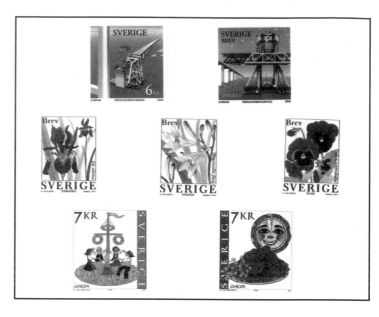

◁ **Swedish money** The main unit of currency is the krona. One hundred öre equal one krona. The 50-krona note shows Jenny Lind, a famous Swedish opera singer. The 20-krona note shows a scene from a story written by Selma Lagerlöf, the first woman to win a Nobel Prize in literature.

SWEDEN

Farmland & Woodland

Mountains

★ Capital

● Major Cities

▲ Mountain Peaks

— Country Boundary

0   25   50   75 Miles
0   50   100 Kilometers

RUSSIA

Arctic Circle

Riksgränsen

Kiruna

Jukkasjärvi

▲ Mt. Kebnekaise

Gällivare

Lule

Pite

Luleå

N O R W E G I A N   S e a

65°N

Skellefte

Vindel

Ume

Umeå

F I N L A N D

L. Kallsjön

Östersund

Örnsköldsvik

L. Storsjön

Inda

Ljungan

Sundsvall

Ljusnan

G u l f   o f   B o t h n i a

Österdal

Västerdal

Siljan

Falun

Gävle

Borlänge

60°N

30°E

Klar

Uppsala

Västerås

L. Mälaren

Mariefred

Karlstad

Eskilstuna

Gulf of Finland

Karlskoga

Örebro

★ **Stockholm**

Söderlälje

RUSSIA

L. Vänern

Motala

ESTONIA

5°E

Uddevalla

Skövde

Norrköping

Göta

Trollhättan

L. Vättern

Linköping

Gränna

Fårö

Göteborg

Borås

Jönköping

Västervik

N o r t h

S k a g e r r a k

Mölndal

Visby

Gotland

L A T V I A

S e a

Falkenberg

L. Bolmen

Växjö

Öland

N

Kattegat

Halmstad

Åsnen

Kalmar

W   E

Helsingborg

Hässleholm

Karlskrona

S

Landskrona

Kristianstad

D E N M A R K

Lund

Hanö Bay

LITHUANIA

55°N

Malmö

Ystad

B a l t i c   S e a

10°E

15°E

20°E

25°E

© Oxford Cartographers

5

WELCOME TO SWEDEN

Sweden is the largest country in northern Europe. It has close historical ties with its neighbors—Norway, Denmark, and Finland. Together, Sweden, Norway, and Denmark make up the region known as Scandinavia.

Sweden is a long, narrow country surrounded on three sides by seas—the North Sea to the west, the Gulf of Bothnia to the east, and the Baltic Sea to the south. There are sandy beaches and rocky cliffs along the coast and many offshore islands. Southern Sweden is mainly flat but rugged. Snow-covered mountains rise above the northern border with Norway. In Sweden's far north, there are forests, swift-flowing rivers, and about 90,000 lakes.

Although Sweden is similar in size to California, only about nine million people live here. Most Swedes—as the people are called—live in the south, near the main cities. They enjoy a prosperous way of life. Schooling and most medical services are paid for by tax-supported government programs, and people who are sick or

▽ **Sweden's great outdoors** Enjoying the peace and beauty of the seashore, lakeside, and mountains is a popular Swedish pastime.

△ **Winter snows in northern Sweden**
Warming winds keep the southern part of the
country less icy, but many southerners head
north for winter snow sports.

◁ **Water festival in Stockholm** In summer,
there are festivals and celebrations all over
the country. Many festivals relate to water
and sea, as lakes, rivers, and the coast are
never far away.

unemployed receive benefit payments. Few
people are poor. Cities are neat and clean,
with modern buildings, as well as old castles
and churches that date back hundreds of
years. Sweden has many modern industries
and well-managed farms. It is a member of
the European Union, a group of fifteen

trading nations. It also has its own king, but
the country is run by government officials
who are elected by the Swedish people.

City-dwelling Swedes love to get away
to explore their countryside. And there is
plenty to explore in this spectacular country,
as you are about to discover.

STOCKHOLM, SWEDEN'S CAPITAL

Sweden's major city is Stockholm. This historic city lies between Lake Mälaren and the Baltic Sea. Stockholm is beautiful, with many parks and areas of water. It is built on fourteen islands. To get from one island to another, you can cross one of fifty bridges or take a ferry. You can also get around the city by bus or by the T-bana subway trains, which carry commuters between the downtown area and the suburbs every day.

Stockholm is the only really big city in Sweden. There are few big factories in the city, but it is Sweden's center of government, education, and communications. Stockholm is the country's second-busiest seaport and has the biggest airport, Arlanda.

Sweden's most important playwright, August Strindberg, was born in Stockholm in 1849. It is also the birthplace of Alfred Nobel, the 19th-century Swedish inventor and industrialist who set up the annual international Nobel Prize awards, which continue to this day.

The picturesque center of Stockholm is the Old Town, which the Swedes call *Gamla Stan*. Here you can visit the Royal Palace, which was built in the 1700s for Swedish kings and queens. Many of Sweden's former kings are buried at Riddarholmen Church, where you can see their tombs. Not far from the Royal Palace is the Riksdag (Swedes say *Reeks-da*) building, where the national parliament meets.

The northern part of Stockholm is the main business district. It is also the best place to go shopping for souvenirs. If, after all that sightseeing, you are feeling hungry and thirsty, head for a café for a drink and an open sandwich, pastry, or salad. Or, go to one of Stockholm's many fine restaurants and help yourself to the tasty hot and cold foods on the *smörgåsbord* table.

▷ **Enjoying the sun and fresh air** In summer, Stockholmers like to meet at outdoor cafés to sip coffee and eat a snack.

◁ **Stockholm's City Hall** This landmark sits on the island of Kungsholmen. Built in 1923, it is called the Stadshuset. Important foreign visitors usually arrive at City Hall by boat.

▽ **Sweden's King Carl Gustaf and Queen Silvia** For the annual ceremonial opening of Parliament, the king and queen ride in a royal carriage from *Gamla Stan* to the Riksdag.

For centuries, Sweden was a great naval power. In Stockholm, the sea is never far away. In a museum by the water is the sailing ship *Vasa*, which was once the pride of Sweden's navy. In 1628, the wooden warship sank, but it was raised from the mud at the bottom of Stockholm Harbor in 1961, preserved, and put on display here.

Sweden's seafaring tradition dates back 1,000 years to the time of the Vikings. In their narrow, wooden longships, the Vikings spread from their Scandinavian homelands to trade, fight, and settle along the coastal regions of Germany, France, and Britain. Vikings from the coast south of Stockholm even sailed to Greenland and North America.

In the eastern part of Stockholm is Djurgården. Now a park, the area used to be the royal family's hunting ground. Today, the park is the site of Skansen, a vast open-air museum. Here, you can see more than 150 reconstructed buildings that date back hundreds of years. They include windmills and farmhouses. Nearby, you can visit Stockholm's zoo and aquarium, or have fun at Tivoli, the city's amusement park.

▷ **The royal palace of Drottningholm** The palace was begun in 1662 and is built in the French style. The palace is open to visitors.

▽ **Viking remains** An ancient stone cross marks the site of the town of Birka, which was once a busy Viking trade center.

Every year in October, Stockholm's sports fans take a ferry to the island of Lidingö. Here, some 30,000 runners compete in the world's largest cross-country race.

On Björkö Island, in Lake Mälaren, you can see the remains of Birka, Sweden's oldest town. One thousand years ago, Vikings lived here. The lake itself has nice beaches.

A pleasant fifty-minute ferry ride from Stockholm will bring you to Drottningholm, Sweden's most elegant palace. You'll find a beautiful theater. Although built in the 1700s, it is still used for plays and concerts.

The tiny village of Mariefred is about an hour west of Stockholm by steamboat. Its streets are lined with traditional wooden houses. From the village, you can take a ride on a restored steam railroad or walk to Gripsholm Castle, which is a reminder of a time when Swedish nobles and kings went to war to protect their country.

▽ **The Lidingöloppet cross-country race**
Athletes from all over the world come to Sweden for the annual event. The race was first held in 1965.

STUDENTS, HISTORY, AND TRADITION

From Stockholm, a fast modern highway going north leads to Uppsala. This busy industrial city is the only big city north of Stockholm. Sweden's largest cathedral, which dates from 1435, is located here. The city is also the home to Sweden's oldest university, which was founded in 1477. Past students of Uppsala University include the botanist Carl von Linné, better known as Linnaeus, and Anders Celsius, the inventor of the Celsius temperature scale.

The sea north of Stockholm is known as the Gulf of Bothnia. To the south is the Baltic Sea. The many fishing villages along Sweden's Baltic coast are popular for vacations and weekend trips during the summer. Swedish law states that people can walk, put up a tent, and pick flowers and berries wherever they like, providing they do not invade a person's privacy or harm the environment.

In the town of Linköping, visit the 13th-century Domkyrkan. (*Domkyrka* is Swedish for cathedral). Its spire rises more than 320 feet (97 m). A smaller neighboring church, St. Lars, has an interesting, though somewhat spooky sight—800-year-old skeletons resting in modern glass coffins. You should also explore *Gamla Linköping*, the old part of the town. Here, you can step back in time. In a restored 19th-century Swedish village, a few people live in old-fashioned buildings and work at traditional crafts.

West of Linköping is Lake Vättern, Sweden's second-largest lake. It is about 80 miles (129 km) long. The lake is very deep, and storms can blow up suddenly. A good stop is Gränna, on the lake's eastern shore. This cute little town is famous for striped candy and hot-air ballooning.

▷ **A feast of fish and seafood** Tasty seafood can be bought from stands in towns and villages. Swedes like eating shrimp, crab, fresh-water crayfish, and raw herring.

◁ **Lowland farms** Good farmland is scarce, except in the southern lowlands. Almost all Swedish farmers form small groups called cooperatives to sell their dairy products, meat, grain, and vegetables.

▽ **Seashore houses** About one in six Swedes live in small wooden houses like these during summer holidays. They are often found in the fishing villages along the coasts.

SUMMER SUN AND ISLANDS

Southern Sweden is flat, and the climate is pleasantly warm in summer. The countryside is ideal for exploring by bicycle. Kalmar and other southern towns are noted for their glass factories, where workers carry on Sweden's proud tradition in art and design.

From Kalmar, a road bridge 4 miles (6.4 km) long connects the mainland with the small island of Öland. Thousands of years ago, prehistoric people settled on the island, and you can still see remains of their forts and burial mounds. Öland's beautiful sandy beaches, windmills, and flower-filled meadows make it a wonderful place for a vacation. It has about seventeen hours of daylight on midsummer days. When you see the beautiful orchids that grow on Öland, it is hard to believe that the island lies in the northern Baltic Sea.

In summer, ferryboats are packed with tourists heading for Öland's larger island neighbor, Gotland, and its capital Visby. As the boat approaches this medieval city, you will see a cathedral rise dramatically from behind the stone walls.

Southern Sweden offers not only pretty sights and sunshine, but also interesting local delicacies. At the old port of Åhus, for example, you can try smoked eels served with scrambled eggs. Frequent fast buses carry people to and from other southern cities, such as Karlskrona, a naval base, and Kristianstad, which is nicknamed Little Paris. In Tivoli Park, you can enjoy waffles and coffee in a 19th-century café and listen to an open-air concert.

At the southern tip of Sweden, the historic town of Ystad has a medieval-style market to explore. A bus trip inland will take you to Hagestad Nature Reserve, which was founded by the great Swedish statesman Dag Hammarskjöld (1905–1961). He was born in Jönköping and became Secretary-General of the United Nations.

◁ **Glassmaking** Swedish glassmakers are highly skilled. Many small glass factories produce items for the tourist trade. The finest glassware is highly prized by art collectors.

▷ **Cathedral towers and city park** Visby's cathedral and medieval area are surrounded by modern houses and parks.

▽ **Medieval pageant** Trumpeters herald the start of family entertainment in Visby, which stages a lively medieval festival in August. People dress up to reenact battles fought against the Danish invaders of 1361.

CLOSE TO DENMARK

The train westward from Ystad travels through the province of Skåne, bound for the city of Malmö. Skåne is known as "the breadbasket of Sweden" because it has the country's best farmland. Farmers grow wheat and vegetables and raise dairy cattle, hogs, and poultry.

Malmö is Sweden's third-largest city. A long sandy beach gives the city its name, which means "sand mound." Malmö is a thriving port for trade between Sweden and the rest of Europe. It has many large office buildings and factories. Among Malmö's attractions are the roller coaster rides at Folkets Park, the oldest amusement park in Sweden. You can also travel along the 10-mile (16-km)-long bridge that links Malmö to the city of Copenhagen in Denmark.

Only 3 miles (4.8 km) of water—called the Öresund (sound)—separate Swedish Helsingborg, to the north of Malmö, from

▽ **On the farm** Dairy farming is an important part of Swedish agriculture. Many farms have a family farmhouse like this one.

△ **Windmills and traditions** Folk dancers keep traditional customs alive in the province of Skåne, where windmills turn in the breeze. Skåne is Sweden's richest farming area.

Helsingør in Denmark. Many young people like to spend a day on a ferry, just for the fun of chatting with friends as the boat chugs back and forth. As the ferry approaches Helsingør, you can see Helsingør Castle. This is the castle that Shakespeare called Elsinore in his famous play *Hamlet*.

Many of the people who pass through Helsingborg take time to wander around Kärnan Fortress, which dates from the 1100s.

Others enjoy the flowers in the elegant Royal Gardens of Sofiero. The garden house, once a king's residence, looks like a railroad station. This is not surprising, since the architect who planned the house in the 1860s designed train stations, too.

▽ **Downtown Malmö** The Rådhus, or City Hall, stands in Malmö's main square. Unlike many city halls, this one has a café in the cellar.

CITY OF CANALS

The stretch of sea off the west coast of southern Sweden is called the Kattegat, Swedish for "cat's throat." On the shores of the Kattegat is the town of Falkenberg, a favorite stopover for fishing enthusiasts. It is on the highway that runs north from Malmö to Göteborg.

Göteborg is Scandinavia's largest seaport and Sweden's second-largest city. In the 1800s, many migrants left from here by ship to settle in the United States. Today, Swedish exports are shipped from this port to all parts of the world, especially to Sweden's European Union trading partners.

Göteborg developed beside the Göta River, and Old Göteborg with its web of canals reminds visitors of a Dutch city. However, the old-time streetcars are all Göteborg's own. A bustling, modern city spreads out around the old section. Take a stroll along the Avenyn, the main street, as there is much to see—shops, restaurants, and museums, including a ship museum complete with a full-size naval destroyer.

Göteborg boasts Sweden's oldest railroad station and a car-making plant as big as a small city—the Volvo Factory. There is a also a Volvo Museum with historic vehicles to interest car enthusiasts. You will find Sweden's biggest shopping mall in Göteborg and the Liseberg Amusement Park, a friendly place for young and old, with bands playing and stomach-churning rides for adventure seekers.

Townsfolk like to buy fresh groceries in the Saluhallen Market or meet friends in one of the city's many small cafés. Eel sandwiches, fresh-baked bread and cheese, and giant cookies made of meringue are among the many good things you'll find to eat.

▷ **International seaport** The harbor of Göteborg handles cargo ships, cruise liners, and ferries. Paper and timber from the northern forests are among the products shipped from here.

18

◁ **Moving around town**
Streetcars are a good way to get around Göteborg. Some of them are more than 90 years old. These old-fashioned cars run in the summer only, but the modern streetcars operate all year round.

▽ **Hero of Göteborg**
A statue of King Gustavus II Adolphus of Sweden stands in Gustav Adolfs Torg (Square). The king founded the city of Göteborg in 1619.

LAKES, DALES, AND SKI RACES

North of Göteborg is the start of the Göta Canal. This waterway was built in the 1800s to link Göteborg to Stockholm, a distance of about 360 miles (580 km). The journey by boat takes about three days. The Göta Canal connects Lake Vänern, Sweden's biggest lake, and the smaller Lake Vättern.

Lake Vänern is Europe's third-largest lake and Scandinavia's largest. Dams have been built on rivers that flow into Lake Vänern to provide hydroelectricity. Sweden gets half its power from hydroelectricity. The rest comes from nuclear-powered or oil-burning plants.

The lake's shores are mostly rocky and forested. At the southern end of the lake, the Göta River tumbled over the falls of Trollhättan, until the waterfall's power was harnessed to produce electricity. The huge floodgates of the power plant are opened in summer for a spectacular water show.

One of the provinces to the north of Lake Vänern is Dalarna, named for the river Dalälven. Here, the town of Falun is famous for its copper mines, but most people come to Dalarna to see the green countryside and to buy such souvenirs as the wooden, red-painted "Dala horses."

In the winter, visitors flock to Dalarna to take part in winter sports. The important ski resorts Sälen and Idre are near the Norway border. Many Swedes like to ski; most prefer long-distance cross-country skiing to high-speed downhill racing.

In Dalarna, as elsewhere in Sweden, winter is also a time for Christmas and New Year celebrations. Christmas is a religious and a family holiday. The festivities begin on December 13, when children led by girls with candle headdresses sing songs to mark St. Lucia's Day.

◁ **Skiing competition** The Vasa Ski Race is held over a 56-mile (90-km)-long course in Dalarna. As many as 14,000 skiers take part in the annual race, which is a test of both fitness and stamina.

△ **A lock on the Göta Canal** Locks raise and lower water levels to allow boats to navigate waterfalls and other obstacles on the canal. There are 58 locks on the Göta Canal.

◁ **The Queen of Light** On St. Lucia Day, girls dress in white and put wreaths on their heads. They carry candles or wear candles on their heads like crowns. The oldest daughter in the family serves drinks and buns for breakfast to other family members.

LIFE IN NORRLAND

Norrland, the northernmost part of Sweden, is where the great outdoors really begins. It is a great place for hiking, skiing, camping, fishing, and mountain-climbing. Although there are few towns, good roads and railroads allow people to travel wherever they want to go.

Very few people live in Norrland, but many who live in the cities farther south keep country cottages in the north that they use for summer vacations.

There are millions of trees here. You will see many wooden houses in the towns and villages along the east coast on the Gulf of Bothnia. In the past, wooden houses often burned—the whole town of Sundsvall burned to the ground in 1888—so most people rebuilt their new homes with stone.

◁ **Over rivers, through forests** This railroad bridge is part of the Inlandsbanan, or "inland railroad." Trains run from the province of Dalarna to Gällivare inside the Arctic Circle.

▽ **On the water** Paddling a kayak is a good way to explore Sweden's waterways. Kayaks can be rented from boating centers.

Swedes call the coast here the High Coast because of its steep cliffs. There are lots of deserted bays and small islands, and it is easy to imagine the Vikings of old setting sail from here in their long ships!

Norrland towns are rich in folklore. Östersund is a town beside Storsjön (the Great Lake), roughly in the center of the country. Visitors here are warned to watch out for the lake's own dog-headed monster!

Like children all over Sweden, northern youngsters attend public schools, which have good facilities for all kinds of sports. Sweden has produced many top-ranking golf, soccer, and tennis stars for the young fans to follow. Swedes love to sing, especially folk songs, and they buy enormous numbers of CDs and cassette tapes to listen to at home or in the car. So many young Swedes dream of being pop stars and/or sports heroes.

▽ **In the wilderness** Hikers in Sweden can reach remote areas by car, bus, train, or bicycle, then follow the trails on foot. They are free to roam anywhere in one of Europe's last unspoiled wildernesses.

LAND OF IRON AND SNOW

The northern towns of Gällivare and Kiruna are famous for their copper and iron mines. Gällivare has the biggest copper mine in Europe. There is gold here, too. Visitors can take a guided tour of modern mines and also see the tumble-down houses where the old-time miners used to live. The other important industry in the north is forestry. The spruce and pine forests provide wood for furniture making and building construction, as well as pulp for paper making.

Here within the Arctic Circle, it feels like a long way from the big cities and open meadows of southern Sweden. High snow-topped mountains rise above deep, cold lakes fed by rushing rivers. Glaciers crunch and grind their way down the mountain slopes. Buildings must be constructed to keep out the freezing winter cold.

People can reach the remote northern towns by plane, car, bus, or by trains that run all the way to the Norwegian border at Riksgränsen. Often, trucks have to stop while elk (large deer similar to the North American moose) wander across the road. Hikers can walk for miles without seeing anyone. They can pitch a tent for the night or stay in a cabin along the well-marked tourist trails. With luck, they will see forest animals, which include red squirrel, roe deer, and Arctic fox. Lynx, brown bear, and wolf are also around, though they are rare.

Winters are long, cold, and dark in northern Sweden. Summers are short. But this is the land of the Midnight Sun, and on Midsummer's Day there are twenty-three hours of daylight. People stay up, dance, and party all through the night. You will find berries and mushrooms to pick—but watch out for buzzing, biting mosquitoes!

◁ **Animal on the move** An elk walks along the water's edge of a northern lake. Elk are common in Sweden's northern forests and often wander across highways.

▷**Wealth from trees** About half the country is covered with trees, mainly conifer. Forestry is efficient and mechanized. The forests are managed either by large corporations or private landowners. Only Canada produces more sawn timber than Sweden.

▽ **Midsummer fun** Summer in Sweden is a welcome break from winter gloom. At the Midsummer Festival, from June 21 to 23, people celebrate the sunshine with Maypole dancing and all-night parties.

LAPLAND

Lapland is a region that extends across northern Scandinavia. It is named for the people who live there, the Lapps. The 17,000 Swedish Lapps, or Sami as they prefer to be called, have their own language and traditional way of life, based on herding reindeer. Most Sami now live in small towns or villages, but some are still nomads, wandering with their reindeer herds. The Sami are skilled at such crafts as sewing and carving. There are also many people of Finnish ancestry in the northland.

There are good trails and overnight cabins to help people explore the large national parks in northern Sweden, such as Padjelanta, the largest park. The best time of year for exploring is between June and September. Hikers must be properly equipped because the weather can be harsh. Detailed maps, a sturdy pair of boots, and a parka to keep out the rain and cold are a must. There is wildlife and wonderful scenery to enjoy, including Sweden's highest mountain, Kebnekaise (Mt. Kebne).

Anyone willing to brave the north in winter can spend a night in an ice hotel! At the town of Jukkasjärvi, this unique hotel, like a giant igloo, is rebuilt every fall from ice. It lasts until the May thaw. In the ice hotel's chilly rooms, guests sleep in special sleeping bags on snow beds covered with reindeer hides. It is a night to remember and an unusual way to end your journey.

△ **Traditional clothes** The colorful traditional clothing of the people of Lapland is made from reindeer skins and wool. Most Sami now wear Western-style clothing much of the time and live and work in towns.

△ **Traveling with the herd** Reindeer provide the Sami with meat, milk, and hides for clothing and tents. The Sami move south with their reindeer herds in winter, returning north in the spring.

▷ **Snowtrek** In winter, skiers can move across country much faster than walkers. The skier glides over the snow with long striding movements, pushing with the poles that are held in the hands.

SWEDEN FACTS AND FIGURES

People

Although most Swedes are born here, 13 percent were born elsewhere. The biggest minority groups are Finns, who speak Finnish as well as Swedish, and Sami, or Lapps, who also have their own language. Other minorities include people who emigrated from southern Europe, Asia, and Africa.

Trade and Industry

Sweden is rich in natural resources. It has huge forests and large deposits of iron, copper, gold, lead, and zinc. Sweden is the world's third-largest exporter of wood pulp and paper. Manufacturing is important, with factories making cars, aircraft, ships, machinery, and electrical appliances. Sweden's main trading partners are Germany, Britain, Denmark, and other members of the European Union. Most working Swedes are employed in service industries, such as health, government, and education.

△ **Insulated from the cold** In the snowy northlands of Sweden, temperatures in winter can stay below 10°F (minus 23°C) for months, so houses must be well heated and insulated.

Farming

Sweden's farms occupy about 10 percent of the land. Farmers raise beef and dairy cattle, hogs, and poultry. Dairy farming is particularly important in the southern provinces. The chief crops are wheat, barley, oats, potatoes, and sugar beets. Some farms are "organic." This means that farmers do not use artificial fertilizers or chemicals on their crops. Also, farm animals are free to graze.

Fishing

Fishing is one of Sweden's lesser industries. Usually, between 300,000 and 400,000 tons of fish are caught each year. Cod, mackerel, and herring are caught in the North Sea. The catch off the Baltic Coast, where the water is less salty, includes a type of herring (*strömming*), pike, pike-perch, sea trout, and salmon. Salmon and other freshwater fish are also taken from Sweden's many lakes and rivers.

Food

Both Swedes and visitors enjoy sampling from the *smörgåsbord*, an assortment of foods such as cold fish (herrings, sardines, shrimp, smoked eels), cold meats (including smoked reindeer meat), hot sausages, omelettes, and bread. Swedes drink lots of coffee and like thick soured milk on their breakfast cereal.

Traditional and popular dishes include:
årtsoppa yellow pea soup
köttbullar Swedish-style meatballs
ostkaka cake made from fresh curds and eggs, served with jelly or berries
plättar thin pancakes, often served as a dessert after the pea soup

Schools
Education is free. Children start school at the age of six or seven and must attend for at least nine years. At 15 or 16, most children go on to upper secondary school for another three years. Many students then continue their education at a college or university. Sweden has some forty institutions of higher education, including thirteen universities.

The Media
Sweden has more than 150 daily newspapers. The two main ones are *Dagens Nyheter* and *Svenska Dagbladet*. There are two TV channels that are run by the state broadcasting authority; a cable channel, which is shared with Norway and Denmark; and a commercial channel (one that carries advertising). Swedish Radio is the state broadcaster, but there are also commercial radio stations across the country.

Architecture
Sweden is full of magnificent buildings in various architectural

△ **Bear family** Sweden has a small number of brown bears that roam the northern forests. They are protected by laws from hunters.

styles from different periods. The 12th-century Cathedral of Lund, with its tall twin towers, was built in the Romanesque style. In 1660, the Swedish architect Nicomedus Tessin the Elder designed the beautiful Kalmar Cathedral in the Italian style. Helsingborg Town Hall dates from 1890 and is in the neo-Gothic style. In the 1920s, the Functionalist style of architecture made use of steel, glass, and concrete.

Art and Drama
Many Swedes take part in local singing and drama groups. There are small theaters all over the country. The Royal Swedish Ballet, founded in 1773, tours the world. Swedish films are also world famous, thanks to the work of such directors as Ingmar Bergman. Ingrid Bergman and Greta Garbo are two famous Hollywood movie stars from Sweden. Traditional folk music has many fans. Sweden's most famous pop band was ABBA, and more recently The Cardigans.

SWEDEN FACTS AND FIGURES

Literature

Swedish literature can be traced back to the sagas, or stories, of Viking times. The most famous Swedish writer is August Strindberg (1849–1912), who wrote plays and novels. Children everywhere have enjoyed the Pippi Longstocking stories of Astrid Lindgren.

Religion

Christianity reached Sweden in A.D. 829, but did not become the main religion until the 1100s. Today, about 87 percent of Swedes belong to the Lutheran Church, but only 10 percent are regular churchgoers. Everyone has freedom of religion.

Festivals

Most festivals are based on the seasons or are religious. Christmas, New Year, Easter, and Whitsun are public holidays. Other festivals include:
April 30 **Valborgsmässoafton** (Walpurgis Night) Bonfires and singing to welcome the spring

△ **Award ceremony in City Hall, Stockholm** Six Nobel Prizes are given each year to distinguished men and women. The prizes were created by the Swedish-born industrialist Alfred Nobel, who invented dynamite in 1867.

June 21-23 **Midsummer** Dancing around the Maypole and partying
August **Moonlight crayfish parties** to mark the end of the summer
December 10 **Nobel Prize Day** Awards ceremony in Stockholm
December 13 **St. Lucia Day** Children sing songs and girls wear candle headdresses to brighten up the dark, cold winter.

Sports

Swedes love outdoor sports. Canoeing, rafting, and salmon fishing are popular in a country with so many lakes, rivers, and canals. Swedes enjoy skiing and horseback riding, as well as soccer, tennis, table tennis, and ice hockey.

Plants

Conifers, such as pine and spruce, cover about half the country. On the mountains, such alpine plants as mosses and lichens grow at higher elevations, while birch trees, heathers, and small shrubs grow at lower elevations.

Animals

Bears, Arctic foxes, lynx, and a few wolves live in northern Sweden. Reindeer herds are kept by the Sami (Lapps), and reindeer roam free across the country. Elk, red deer, and roe deer are common in central and southern Sweden. Sweden's rich birdlife includes gulls, terns, and eider ducks on the coasts, eagles in the forests, and cranes in the northern marshland.

HISTORY

People first settled in Sweden about 8,000 years ago, when the Ice Age ended in northern Europe. About 2,000 years ago, the Romans knew about a people they called the "Sveari." (Today, Swedes call their country "Sverige.")

Christianity was brought to Sweden by missionaries in A.D. 829, but it took time to replace the old pagan beliefs of the Vikings, whose journeys from Sweden took them to America.

In 1397, Sweden, Denmark, and Norway were united as one kingdom. Sweden broke away in 1523, and its leader, Gustavus Vasa, became king. In the 1630s, King Gustavus Adolphus led Swedish armies to victories that made Sweden a great power in northern Europe. That power ended in 1709. Sweden was defeated by Russia and was forced to give up most of its foreign territories. Norway came under Swedish rule in 1814, after Sweden helped to defeat France and Denmark in the Napoleonic Wars.

During the 1800s, about a million Swedes emigrated to the United States to escape poverty at home. Later, Sweden became more industrialized. New laws limited the king's power and provided free benefits and services to all of the people.

In 1905, Norway gained independence from Sweden. Sweden stayed neutral in World War I (1914–1918) and World War II (1939–1945). The usually nonviolent country was shocked by the murder of prime minister Olof Palme in 1986. In 1995, Sweden joined the European Union, a group of countries closely linked together by trade.

LANGUAGE

Swedish, like Norwegian and Danish, belongs to the North Germanic group of languages. Its grammar and vocabulary are rather like German. Swedes speak their language in a singsong way that is not easy for a foreigner to master. Also, some vowels are pronounced in a way unfamiliar to English-speakers. Examples are y as in ewe and u as in fur. In Swedish, days and months do not start with capital letters, as they do in English.

Useful words and phrases

English	Swedish
one	ett
two	två
three	tre
four	fyra
five	fem
six	sex
seven	sju
eight	åtta
nine	nio
ten	tio
Sunday	söndag
Monday	måndag

Useful words and phrases

English	Swedish
Tuesday	tisdag
Wednesday	onsdag
Thursday	torsdag
Friday	fredag
Saturday	lördag
Good morning	god morgon
Good night	god natt
Yes	ja
No	nej
Thank you/Please	tack
Do you speak English?	talar du engelska?

INDEX

Acknowledgments
Book created for Highlights for Children, Inc.
by Bender Richardson White.
Editors: Belinda Weber, Mike March, and Lionel Bender
Designer: Mike Pilley, Radius Graphics
Art Editor: Ben White
Picture Researcher: Cathy Stastny
Production: Kim Richardson

Maps produced by Oxford Cartographers, England.
Banknotes from Thomas Cook Currency Services.
Stamps from Stanley Gibbons.

Editorial Consultant: Andrew Gutelle
Guide to Sweden is approved by the Swedish Tourist Office, London
Swedish Consultant: Gunilla Borén
Managing Editor, Highlights New Products: Margie Hayes Richmond

Picture credits
EU = Eye Ubiquitous, RH = Robert Harding, SIS = Stockholm Information Service, JDTP = James Davis Travel
Photography. t = top, b = bottom, l = left, r = right.
Cover: SIS/R. Ryan. Pages 6, 7t: RH/Christer Andréason. 7b, 8: SIS/R. Ryan. 9t: EU/Hans Nelsäter. 9b: SIS/R. Ryan.
10: EU/Hans Nelsäter. 10-11: Camera Press. 11b: EU/Hans Nelsäter. 12-13: Robert Harding. 13t: EU/Hans
Nelsäter. 13b: JDTP. 14: Life File Ltd. 15t: EU/Märten Adolfson. 15b: Robert Harding. 16l: Liam White
Photography. 16r: EU/Book Magazine Press. 17: EU/The Picture Store. 18-19t: EU/Hans Nelsäter. 18-19b:
EU/Bengt Andréasson. 19: Robert Harding/Julia Thorne. 20, 20-21, 21: EU/Hans Nelsäter. 22t: EU/Bengt
Andréasson. 22b: Robert Harding/Kim Hart. 23: EU/Hans Nelsäter. 24: EU/Roland Svensson. 25t, 25b: EU/Jens
Thuresson. 26: David Simson/DAS Photos. 27t: EU/Jens Thuresson. 27b: Stockmarket/Zefa/Stoecklein. 28: JDTP.
29: Oxford Scientific Films/Martyn Chillmaid. 30: SIS/L. Åstrom. *Illustration on page 1* by Tom Powers.